About the Author

S. Mile lives in Ontario, Canada. She is a full-time educator and activist. In her free time, she likes to travel and explore nature's sights around the world. Her cat, Pepi, is her best teacher and favorite philosopher.

Child in Chaos

S. Mile

Child in Chaos

Olympia Publishers
London

www.olympiapublishers.com
OLYMPIA PAPERBACK EDITION

A CIP catalogue record for this title is
available from the British Library.

ISBN: 978-1-80439-979-8

This book is a memoir. It reflects the author's present recollections of
experiences over time. Some names and characteristics have been
changed, some events have been compressed, and some dialogue
has been recreated.

First Published in 2024

Olympia Publishers
Tallis House
2 Tallis Street
London
EC4Y 0AB

Printed in Great Britain

Dedication

I dedicate this work to all the children of war. May you share your own stories with the world.

Acknowledgments

I want to thank foremost my immediate and extended family for retelling me our story again and again throughout the years in Canada and while visiting Bosnia and Herzegovina. Secondly, I want to thank my friends for their support during this writing process. You have listened to me express my feelings and thoughts without judgment – only understanding and compassion. Thirdly, I want to thank my cat Pepi for sitting beside me while I was typing the words and purring away as I continued for hours on end.

Who are we without our memories?

1. EARLY YEARS / PRE-WAR

I
The Little Rebel

My first act of rebellion started in the womb. My mother's due date was November fifteenth. I was born eleven days later. Unlike my sister, who was delivered easily in the back of a car, my mother had several pregnancy complications with me, and, in the end, she needed to be infused in order to give birth to me. I like to think of it as my reluctance to enter into this realm or reality. Did my unborn self-know something that my born self never could?

There are photos of me celebrating my first birthday in a brown and violet dress. Short blonde hair and hazel eyes. I definitely do not look impressed, by any means. In fact, I look puzzled by the large cake in front of me. The first three years, my mother dressed me up in the prettiest dresses (according to her) and styled my hair in various fashions.

It was at the age of four that I refused to wear the clothes she picked out for me, and, fortunately, my father supported my decision to choose my own style. I remember specific instances of following my father to the bathroom, and I would watch him put shaving cream on his face and take his razor, removing all the hair on his face. I was so fascinated by this. In fact, one day I went into the bathroom while my parents and my sister were watching TV, took the shaving cream and razor out of the bathroom cabinet, and decided to shave my face like my father. Instead of putting a good amount of shaving cream on, I only put a small layer on my face, forgetting to pass the razor through running water. I placed it on the left side of my jaw and cut myself deeply. I still have this scar thirty-three years later. It often reminds me of a quote said by the fictional character Hannibal Lecter: "Our scars have the power to remind us that our past was real."

I was somewhat of a shy child, especially around adults. Visiting other adults with my parents, I always felt like it was punishment. I would constantly need to find ways to entertain myself, and sometimes the adults would let me watch something on TV to pass the time. One evening in 1990, my parents were visiting their best friends, and the hostess, Esma, allowed me to watch this black-and-white movie called *King Kong*. I was glued to the TV, and when I saw that it was a big gorilla—the size of a building—I ran into the kitchen and hid myself (the adults did not notice) because I saw that the young woman in the movie was blonde, and because I am blonde, I thought King Kong would come for me too. Child logic. Even years later, when I became older, I still had some anxiety watching *King Kong*, strangely enough.

In regards to my sister, who is eight years older, I observed her closely growing up. She was a big influence on me when it came to music, art, and behavior. I listened to a lot of the music she did: Nirvana, Metallica, and other rock and metal bands. I also learned how to play pool. Without anybody knowing, I stole a few of her cigarettes one day and smoked them outside of the apartment building. The brand name was VEK. She had many interesting friends that came to visit us on weekends. I am not sure why I did this, but, every time they came over, I would disturb them, jump on them, and hit them with a wooden bat. My sister, on many occasions, tied me to a radiator because I was impossible to deal with. I loved creating chaos wherever I went.

II
Mia

The back of our apartment building was my heaven and my hell. It was the place where all the children in the neighboring buildings would come and play together. It started off as innocent marble and tag play, but later we formed our little gangs and fought each other in battles of rock throwing, kicking, and pistol duels. I had this long blue pistol that I would carry at the side of my jeans every day that I met up with the rest of the kids. My father's plaid and flannel collection soon became 'mine', as my mother would purchase mini-sized plaid and flannel shirts for me. I loved wearing them with my jeans and boots. I also demanded that I get a mushroom haircut to accompany my 'cowboy' mannerisms. Looking back on it at the age of thirty-three, I knew that I was different than most other girls my age. Actually, many girls my age stayed home and played with their dolls. I, on the other hand, made friends with mostly boys and another girl, Mia. Mia was a light brunette, and she also sported a mushroom haircut. I remember her fawn-like eyes—they were a lovely shade of brown. Every time she smiled, her eyes would light up the room.

My friend Ivan, a skinny boy with big round glasses, was the first person to introduce me to her. I knew that Ivan mentioned her on several occasions because she just recently moved into his building. Apartment 305, to be exact. When I saw Mia outside of their building, I felt my body react in a strange way, and my stomach was acting up too. I got nervous and a bit perplexed as I said hello and introduced myself. Mia smiled at us and said that she was happy to meet other kids her age as she left all her old friends in Jajce, another Bosnian town. I did not mind having another friend besides Ivan, and, after three months, we became the three amigos, or the three 'cowboys.'

After spending so much time together—we were all five years old—I started developing romantic feelings for Mia as the days went by. I specifically recall the time I listened to my favorite artist, Dino Merlin, and the song 'Mjesecina' (Moonlight) would come on. It immediately made me fantasize about Mia's beautiful face and the way she would laugh. She had a peculiar laugh—it would start off quiet and then accelerate, and then she would not be able to stop herself, infecting us with her laughter. Her personality was just as rebellious as mine, and Ivan would be the one who would tell us to not do something or to think about the consequences of our actions. He was the rational one, most definitely.

Since we could only see and play with each other on Saturdays, I would impatiently be asking my sister which day it was. I am sure she got annoyed with me many times during the week. I was so joyous knowing that Saturday had arrived. I would style my hair, pick out my clothes, and put shoes on. I would then run down the stairs to the back door and walk slowly, observing my environment, to Ivan and Mia's building. I knew where their balconies were, and I would watch patiently. Since Mia was a big part of that joy, I would shout her name, and sometimes she would step out onto the balcony and tell me she would be right there, and at times she would throw down her toys, and I would catch them in my arms. This is still one of the fondest memories I have before the war in Bosnia and Herzegovina.

The three of us lived in our own little world, forgetting our surroundings and the curfew time, only to have our angry parents looking for us and shaking their fingers as we would accompany them back. There was an old train track and an abandoned locomotive past our buildings, a ten-to-fifteen-minute walk, where we would go exploring. Sometimes, we would go inside the cabins and collect rocks and pull out the weeds. We would bring our toys up there and pretend we would have tea, making it our third home. At times, I would go by myself if Ivan and Mia couldn't, for whatever reason. I would see rabbits inside the cabins, birds, and carcasses, which fascinated me. I am grateful to my parents for trusting me at an early age. Our town of Vareš was a small town, and everyone knew each other, so there was no fear of being kidnapped, raped, or killed by a stranger. I had a lot more freedom looking back than most kids today. I treasure that sense of freedom more than anything.

There were two new families that moved into our building, and they had five boys combined. The boys were a bit older than us and would act like they were the bosses of us. Ivan would be the chosen target of bullying, while Mia and I were ignored because we were girls. We stood up to them and threw rocks back at them. In fact, one day we decided we would all (along with other kids in the neighborhood) have a car jumping competition. Yes, a car jumping competition which involved just that: jumping over cars. I think it was Mia's idea, as she saw it in an action movie. So, of course, we had to test the theory! We all lined up in a straight line, and we waited our turn to jump over a set of six to seven cars. Everyone succeeded except for me! As I reached midway, my foot fell through the windshield, and I got stuck in it. Ivan and two other boys helped get me out. As we noticed what had happened, we all ran home in order to avoid the severe consequences. About an hour later or so, my parents received a knock at the door. One of the dads came by with his son and told my dad what had happened. I still can hear my dad's words: "My little angel?"

"Yes, sir," replied the man. My parents had to pay two hundred KM for the damage, and I received some spanking that night and was grounded for a week or so. No more car jumping competitions after that!

It wasn't long after this incident that Mia and her family moved to Tuzla. Her father received a better job offer, and they already had some family living there. When Ivan told me that Mia only had four days left with us before she moved away and began a new journey, I did not waste any time hanging out with her and even had my mom buy flowers for the family as a good-bye gift. I never ended up telling her how I felt, but I did kiss her cheek and watch her drive away in her family car, waving back at her. I shed many tears afterward in my room for days and days to come. I still declare openly to this day that Mia was my first love and that without her, in some ways, I would never have known the meaning of romance and the joys of innocent courtship.

III
Relaxation

My father, from an early age, became interested in alternate methods of healing such as bio-energy, acupressure, and Eastern medicine. Once a week, he would ask my sister and me to join him for a relaxation session. These relaxation sessions involved a tape being played on a recorder—a soft, feminine voice that would take us step-by-step into a deep, relaxed state of mind. She would tell us to lie down, lift one arm at a time, and release them at a slow pace, breathing in and out. I felt like I would be 'out' of my body and my mind being silent. After the tape ended, my father would do his own small session by placing his hands on our hands and then lifting them up about two cm and slowly staying in a particular area. My sister kept saying that she would feel such warmth close to her heart and also her whole body would be working simultaneously, directing that warmth everywhere. Often times, I would fall asleep during and after the session, and my father or my mother would just carry me into bed. I looked forward every week to this practice, and it really came in handy later, when our world as we knew it would change forever.

Being in nature by myself was something that I found to be profoundly healing. I became mesmerized by all the colors I would see around me—in living things such as the birch trees, which are the most common trees in Bosnia and Herzegovina. You could observe the different shades of white and gray and the different patterns each tree would display to show its uniqueness. Even when we escaped our city of Vareš while the war was still happening and took refuge in the small town of Volujak (a separate chapter later in the memoir), I would walk into the nearby forest and collect empty bullet shells. Sometimes, I would find a full shell and bring it home to show my family. I had a whole bag of different models. I remember just being in the moment and not fearing anything or anyone. Life for me was still beautiful despite its ugliness.

As I mentioned earlier in another chapter, the train tracks were a place of imaginary travel where one could be anywhere one wanted to be by just creating images in the mind and letting them transport the 'traveler' to their chosen destination. My father would accompany me sometimes when he did not have other responsibilities at home, and we would play hide and seek for an hour or two. I told him that I wanted to become a train conductor when I grew up and that I would take all my friends and all the animals in the abandoned locomotive. I wish we did not lose the photos of the abandoned locomotive where my father would take my sister and me several times a year. It was a hauntingly magnificent place, and we would all wonder who was on this locomotive and what their life story was. There was some graffiti on the side doors, but it did not really make any sense to us. I carved my name into the rusty parchment with a Swiss army knife, and I wonder if it is still there after all these years.

IV
Goran

My uncle Goran was a giant of a man standing close to two meters. He had dark, curly hair and a well-kept goatee. He was the husband of my mother's youngest sister, Dražana. He was also the father of two young boys, one aged eight and the other eight months. Goran was known as a troublemaker in his teens and young adult years. He was a restless soul, searching for new experiences every chance he got. He used to say that in order to fully experience life, one has to try everything at least once! He lived by what he preached. I do not think anyone who knew him would disagree with that.

Some of the memories that I have of him as a child involve being outside and doing things. Being active, whether going for long walks or playing sports, strengthened one's sense of self, and Goran was one of the most confident people in our town. He was also extremely charming and had a distinct walk. Goran was fascinated by philosophy, particularly metaphysics. My family used to hide the fact that he drank quite a bit and did drugs, mostly marijuana, which was such a taboo back then. Still is, if I am to be completely honest. I really saw him as an embodiment of 1960s counterculture and the hippy movement. A Bosnian hippy in his own right.

For my fourth birthday, he bought a second-hand Formula car for me because he knew I preferred toys that boys had. This black Formula had pedals on it and such a cool exterior—all black with a bit of silver for an extra touch. I remember 'driving' it everywhere across town with my dad following in the back. It was an unforgettable experience every time I got into this machine. I always felt Goran knew me more than anyone else did. He was such a strong role model for me, and I loved that he questioned everything around him, whether it be mainstream religion or politics.

Goran got involved with the army in his twenties, and he defended Bosnia and Herzegovina from the Bosniak invasion in the 1990s. He got a peace tattoo on his hand soon after becoming a soldier—close to his thumb. Every time I see a peace symbol, it always makes me think of him. I wish we had more time together, but unfortunately, Goran was taken from all of us by a grenade that shattered his body on the fields (described by one of his army buddies) at the age of thirty. Now he only lives on in our memories.

V
Freddie Mercury

British rock bands were popular back home, and one of the most listened to was Queen. I heard about them through my sister, whose friends had a diverse collection of tapes and records. I remember the cover of their first debut album. The colors purple and pink dominated the eyes, and the spotlight on a male figure with his arms raised high and holding a microphone were short of hypnotizing. I stared at it for long periods of time, wondering about this male figure who seemed like a hero or a god figure.

I asked my sister's friend to play it for me, and she did. When I heard the voice of the lead singer, I immediately asked whose voice that was, and she told me that it was Freddie Mercury. Freddie Mercury? Freddie Mercury. She showed me a photo of the band in a music magazine. "This must be him," I said.

"Yes, that's him."

I saw a man with beautiful dark brown eyes and dark hair. I could not help but notice his groomed moustache. It suited him! At that moment, I fell in love with him. He had a mystery about him and a soft demeanor, which appealed to me. He also wore pink in the photo, which was not something I saw other men wear in town or in popular culture.

One Sunday afternoon, while my mother and I were visiting our local piazza (market), I saw that Queen was on the cover of a magazine, and I begged her to buy me the magazine. She did but wondered what I would do with it since I was still unable to read and not even in school yet. I still convinced her that I enjoyed the photos and that my sister would probably want to read it too (an excuse – my sister never even opened the magazine!). My obsession with Queen continued for months after that. I knew how to sing the songs 'I want to break free' and 'We Are the Champions' by heart, even though I had no idea what they meant until I learned to speak English in Ontario, Canada. I did the same with many other foreign bands, such as Guns n' Roses, Nirvana, and Bon Jovi. My love for these bands is still very much alive today, but with less intensity!

The confidence and flamboyance that Freddie showed in every one of his performances were captivating for most people. His outfits, his 'feminine' ways, his voice, and his good looks made him interesting and different than other artists. He brought so much joy to many people, especially those who felt like outcasts most of their lives. It was only in my teens that I realized I did not belong to the mainstream way of thinking or acting, and because of that, I was bullied for many years and fell into a deep state of despair and melancholy. I was able to get myself through many tragic episodes with the help of music and the artists' lives I truly admired.

It was at my grandmother's apartment that I found out that Freddie Mercury died of AIDS. I did not know what AIDS was or the reason behind his death because 'homosexual' and 'AIDS' were not words anyone spoke about in my family. When the radio host played one of the Queen's songs, I started sobbing uncontrollably on the floor of my grandmother's kitchen, and she had to call my parents so they could calm me down. I did not understand that someone could just die and never be seen again performing or anything. It was my first experience of grief ever because nobody before that died that I cared so much about. Little did I know that my grief would continue that year and for many years to come.

VI
Marshall Tito

Josip Broz dobar skroz was a popular T-shirt back in the 1990s worn by former partisans, and, in some places in Bosnia, you can still see some people wearing them—usually the boomer generation. When we were still in Vareš, my grandparents (mother's side) had a portrait of Josip Broz Tito in their home. I remember the reddish and gold paint and Tito in his Marshall uniform looking to the left side. I did not know much about him other than my parents raving about the good old days and how now everyone was divided. Tito died on fourth May 1980, two years after my sister was born. Without going into too much of the history of his presidency, Tito was revered by many in Yugoslavia (Socialist Federal Republic of Yugoslavia) as a benevolent ruler. Often times, even in 2020, one can hear stories about Tito in the capital of Sarajevo, as well as the smaller villages in the country. The nationalists would always condemn him and declare him a dictator, so if the reader wants to know more about him, please do not hesitate to look him up and do read more than one book on the man!

Despite his controversial presidency (depending on who you ask!), Tito was, without a doubt, a man who fought against fascism in all its forms and was a defender of the people. '*Smrt fašizmu, sloboda narodu*' was a phrase Yugoslavia was founded on. Tito defended his socialist republic against Stalin, and he greatly influenced Mao's China. Stalin tried to assassinate him many times but failed miserably. Tito, in response (in a letter), told him that he would only need to send one man, and that would be it. I asked my grandmother to read me some of the newspaper articles that she kept over the years so I could understand this man and his popularity. This helped me see what the appeal was, and, honestly, I cannot blame anyone for putting this man on a pedestal. When he died in 1980, he had the largest funeral out of any president, dead or alive. People stood out on the streets for hours, women crying and holding candles and flowers. Prime ministers and presidents from all around the world sent him their condolences, even the Queen of England liked the man.

Why did I choose to dedicate a chapter to Tito in this short memoir? I couldn't not. This man sacrificed so much for his people, and what he preached was brotherhood and unity. Bratstvo i jedinstvo in Serbo-Croatian. Yugoslavia was a prosperous country under him. Other nations looked up to us and appreciated the partisan efforts during WWII. I sometimes wonder what my birth country would have been like if Hitler ended up winning the war. What a revolting and disturbing thought! I am grateful for all my family's stories about this man, even the stories that saw him as a negative figure. Not everyone in my extended family were Communists or whatever you want to call them (some argue that Socialists is a better term). Some abruptly supported and still support the nationalist parties and their agendas, while others are nostalgic about the past, like my parents and many other people in the Balkans.

2. WAR

VII
The Sirens

Two months before the war broke out in 1991, we had practice drills in Vareš almost every evening. I still remember the sounds—loud and unnerving. My mother would have packed us a ready-to-go suitcase with our belongings as my father would converse with our neighbors. The drills would start at one a.m. and end at two a.m. I knew that they were important, but as a five-year-old child, I did not fully comprehend the entire situation. There was only so much my little mind could relate to. My sister told me on one occasion how Mom and Dad were constantly talking about the politics in the country and what would it mean if their chosen representative did not win. How severe would the consequences be? If you ask many people now if they knew a war would break out, they would say no. They still held to their naivete and their brotherhood ideals of unity and respect. On the other hand, there were others who could not wait for the war to happen (a.k.a., nationalists of all parties).

One November evening, an older gentleman in a military uniform came to our front door and asked if there were any men in the home. My mother answered nervously with a yes, and then the man wearing an HVO uniform (a Bosnian Croat) stormed in and looked around the apartment. My sister and I were scared because we knew the reason he came: to take our beloved father to war. My father appeared out of the bedroom and said that he will do what he must. At that exact moment, my mother fell to the ground and pleaded with the military officer not to take him away. She cried in a way unlike any of us had seen before. How could she not? The officer firmly stated that my father would receive a blue uniform tomorrow, delivered by a lower-rank officer. He had three days to spend with us, and then they would come for him and take him to a nearby village.

I can still see my father if I close my eyes in his blue uniform with a hat marked with HVO, so he could be identified as a Bosnian Croat by the other soldiers. Those three days we spent together before my father's departure to war are a distant memory. There was a lot of cuddling and sleeping together—all four of us on one bed. We did not get much sleep in those last two months with the constant sirens going off and people running around their apartments. The walls were thin, so we could even hear people crying and yelling, sometimes at the same time.

When the day came for the officers to take my father away, I knew that maybe I would never see my father again. I remember his face smiling at us and telling us that things would be okay. My mother held us as he exited the apartment building with the officers. I ran to the window to see which car they were taking him in and to take one last glimpse of my father's face. My mother and sister held each other, crying, as I stood there watching and asking why this was all happening.

VIII
The Screams

With my father gone, my mother and my sister remained vigilant during the weeks that followed. My mother's aunt's son remained hidden in his room; he was eighteen at the time, and Marta (his mother) kept him in another room for weeks so that the HVO officers would not come for him. They needed more men to fight in the war, so they kept circling around the city to find every last one of them. Our neighbor Aida, also my mother's friend, suffered at the hands of HVO soldiers who were taking out their rage on Bosniaks for killing their own.

We all could hear her screams late in the evening. They first beat her husband, who was a Muslim, and then killed him in front of her and her children. Later, as we could hear (their apartment was on top of ours), there was a lot of screaming and things being thrown around; after that evening, none of us could sleep for days. We never saw or heard from Aida and her children again. My mother was certain that the gunshots she heard after we fell asleep that evening were from Aida's apartment. Neither of us spoke about what we heard or mentioned Aida's name again.

The bombs and gunshots were the only music in our city for months on end. After weeks of anxiety and terror, I somehow got used to it, and it seemed like a normal occurrence. There was a bomb that exploded in front of our apartment building, and the buildings across from us were covered with bullets. My sister usually kept the blinds closed, and we were never to go near the windows. We were to stay in the center of the apartment, close to the bathroom. It was the safest place to be. We had our bed right in the middle of it all. My mother would prepare quick meals for us—usually polenta and some milk. Sometimes an apple—this food was gathered before the war started, just in case. We were okay for a while.

The first encounter with death, if I can use that word, was when we received a knock on the door one mid-afternoon. My mother told my sister and me to go to the bathroom. My sister put me on her lap while she was on the closed toilet seat. I was so scared that I kept shivering and shaking uncontrollably. My sister remained composed even though she was terrified too. She did it for me and for my mother. My mother bravely went to the door and unlocked it. In front of her, as she described it to us, was a soldier with an unmarked affiliation. He asked for her name and how many people she had inside. She said, "Silvana Miletovic. My name is Silvana Miletovic, and I have my two daughters with me."

To that, he replied, "Okay, Silvana. I am in the Bosnian Croatian army, and I am asking you to keep the door locked and do not open the door for anyone else, you understand?" Then he left.

After my mother closed the door, my sister and I ran up to her and held her, and we all started to cry, but this time it was a cry of relief. We had our mother with us. She was not taken from us like our father. We were safe. My mother – our protector.

IX
The Army Trucks

That same year, we received news that several army trucks would arrive in Vareš to gather all the women and children and bring them to a secure location. We weren't sure what to think of this, but what choice did we really have? Knowing that our town would be taken over by the Bosniak army, most families decided that stepping into the unknown was less frightening than facing the wrath of another hateful group. So, that very night, my mother packed a bag of clothes for all three of us and some leftover money that she kept for emergencies—the equivalent of twenty Canadian dollars. We still had some food as well to keep us going for at least another week.

Soon after (approximately four to five days), we took all our belongings and exited the building. There were large crowds of other women and children—some elderly folk—in the streets lined up, while further in the distance we could see three large army trucks with some men carrying rifles and Kalashnikovs. My mother tried to spot other people she knew in the line-up (mainly my grandmother and my grandfather), as well as her sisters and their children. For the longest time, we did not see or hear from one another. The phone lines were cut, and it wasn't exactly safe to go out in the streets while the bombs were going off and people were shooting each other.

We got loaded on the second truck with other families. There were so many of us that we could not even breathe properly. My mother secured us a corner close to the trunk, and we just sat on the floor and looked back as the truck departed. My sister cried as we looked back on our apartment building and the city we had treasured for so long. Each truck had two men looking after us. They gave the mothers some bread and water for the children; they did not have much either. I remember an hour into the drive I had to pee, and obviously they would not stop for that, so I ended up peeing in at the back of the truck (the trunk was open while the truck was still moving) – it was the only way they allowed people to pee. The men would stand up and pee into the road in front of them. The women mostly waited. Fortunately, they did allow us one ten-minute pit stop finally since so many of the women complained. We used this ten-minute pit stop to go pee and shit behind the bushes and trees. Such relief when people were able to do that!

Soon after, we came close to a 'border'—a Serbian border. The men on the truck told us to stay quiet and that they would try to negotiate with the guards to let us through. I could see the anxiety and panic on people's faces as the men got off the truck and proceeded to negotiate. "What if they refuse to let us pass? What will we do then?" By the grace of God, as some would say, they gave us the green light and even made sure we had more water on the trucks. We got lucky! Maybe it was because there were mainly women and children on the trucks, or maybe it was because they too had mothers, sisters, and children of their own. We will never know the true reason, but we will never forget the Serbian soldiers who ensured our safety and lives! They did not ask for our names or anything like that. There were Bosnian Croats and Bosnian Serbs on the trucks. We united together in our fear, our strength, and our familial bonds. One big family desperate to survive and keep on surviving.

X
Homelessness

Shortly after crossing the Serbian border, we found ourselves on a large green field with a small house overlooking the forest area. All of the three trucks parked in the middle of the green field, and, there, all of the families from our city dispersed, looking for their other family members and friends. My sister saw our grandparents as well as our mom's sisters and their sons. The reunion—there are no words to describe what we felt when we all came together. I will not bother with it.

The men in charge told us that this was where we would be 'camping' for the next two weeks until they find another option. This area was well guarded by Bosnian Serbs, and it was the safest place to be for now. We accepted our fate and tried to make the best of it for the time being. The weather got colder as the days passed by. Some people had extra blankets to keep themselves warm, and some slept just in their clothes. There was no place to wash up or to go to the toilet. The forest and the ponds were the replacements for that once-domestic privilege. We were the people of the green field—that's what people would say at night. A people without a city, a people without a home to call their own any more.

In the small house mentioned before, there lived a middle-aged Bosnian Serb couple who opened their home to young mothers and their small children when the weather got too cold. I remember my mother and I, along with my aunts and their little boys, spending three nights inside. It was marvelous, and we would sleep through anything! The lady did not have much, but she was kind and compassionate. My grandfather gave his last ten KM to the lady so she could bake a big loaf of bread for us to eat. We were beyond grateful. Sometimes, she would heat up some milk for all the children (they had cows), and it would be the most delicious treat any one of us could ask for!

My sister and my grandparents slept outside for two weeks in the cold and in the pouring rain. At one point, my sister got sick, and she needed medications to treat her cold (respiratory issues). She was helped by another family who had a small pack of antibiotics or something of that sort. I do not recall what the exact pills were. It does not matter. The brutal conditions were enough to affect the body in a negative way.

We all tried to make the best of it, and I think we got quickly accustomed to a daily routine of getting up, heading to the forest to do our 'business,' collecting wood for a nice fire in the evenings, and partaking in conversations and meal sharing. As I said earlier, we became one big family, taking care of each other and leaving any differences behind. People that never spoke to each other in the city became fast friends, and, for us kids, we played with each other and were genuinely happy for a while. The fact that we were still alive pushed us to live life to the fullest, knowing the fact that life is short. The darkness shall pass, and brighter days are yet to come. And with this belief system in place, the brighter days did come.

XI
Volujak

'Once a refugee, always a refugee' was a common saying amongst the people. Displacement was a hard pill to swallow for many during the war. Leaving our homes, the cities, and villages we grew up in, not to mention the separation of loved ones, was something that took years to accept. Our reality as we had imagined it was stripped from us, and we had to replace it with something—anything to fill that void. As we left the camp, the men in charge told us they would be taking us to three different places (all occupied by the Croatian army). These places were safe for all of us, as the Bosniak army was not as powerful there. The Croatian army defended these places with all their might and secured its sovereignty, if I can use that precise wording.

The place that we were supposed to settle in is named Volujak. Vol means just like in French (fly), and jak stands for strong. The flying strong! It seemed somewhat fitting in the way that it gave us some renewed hope that once we settled there, we could rebuild our lives again. My aunts and their sons, as well as my grandfather and grandmother, were in a place called Kiseljak and Kreševo, while the people on our truck settled in Volujak (as stated previously). They were all about a ten-to-fifteen-minute drive from each other, so it was not that bad. Most days, we walked to see the rest of our family.

Everyone had a house of their own (donated by the kind people from those places)—it was nothing fancy. Quite small actually, but it was better than not having any shelter. We were beyond grateful, and we expressed it by cooking for the owners and also working on their fields. My mother would spend the whole day (sixteen hours or so) working on the fields. She would get paid by being given food, and if the owners had some spare money, they would give her ten KM (seven Canadian dollars) per day for her hard work. I remember my mother treating us to ice cream sometimes on Saturdays. There was so much joy for both my sister and me. We definitely appreciated those small moments of happiness.

So, here we were, in a new place, struggling to make it work. The two women (also sisters) that let us have their spare house were very gentle. They would bring us fresh milk every other day and would invite us for dinner as well on the weekend. My mother became close friends with them. Both of them were unmarried and lived together in Volujak all their lives. Ana and Danica – their names. I remember Ana being the funny one most of the time, while Danica was mostly serious. Ana would bring cards and some wine sometimes to our place, and we would play cards with them. Well, they would play cards; I would watch and keep score. Danica was a master strategist; she was able to come up with amazing plans and solutions to pretty much everything. Kind of like a jack-of-all-trades. There was nothing that that woman could not do.

I remember vividly one day when Ana brought us a used TV My sister and I were so happy. There was an antenna that could capture three channels, one of them was a soap opera (TV shows station in English), and the other two were news and nature channels. I remember we had to tape the antenna closer to the window so we could catch all the channels; if it moved even slightly, the screen would disappear. We spent so much time getting up and adjusting the antenna until we finally found the best angle for it. My sister and I watched two specific TV shows: *Beverly Hills 90210* and *Santa Barbara*. We fell in love with the characters and their drama, which distracted us from our own emotional stress. We could focus finally on other people instead of always being and staying in our heads for long periods of time.

XII
The Beheaded Bosniak Soldiers

To celebrate their victories in the war, the Croatian army would behead the Bosniak soldiers and kick their heads down the main road in Kiseljak. My sister was there the second time it happened. She was enrolling herself at the local high school that day. There was a bus from Volujak to Kiseljak a few times per day, so she decided to take matters into her own hands. I am not sure what she felt after she saw heads rolling down the main road. I can only imagine what had been going through her mind.

She told my mother and me when she got home, skipping all the gruesome details, but it was enough for someone to say that there were dead bodies without heads being thrown on the side of the road. There was no burial or any respect for them. Eventually, the bodies were removed from the original place and, I guess, thrown elsewhere. Dead bodies start to decompose pretty quickly in the summer months, and, flies and insects, as well as hungry dogs and cats, would pick at them.

It was well known from a friend of ours who served in the Croatian army that the soldiers would make necklaces of their victims' teeth and wear them proudly out in public. Sometimes, they would compete with each other to see how many one could collect. To be honest, all soldiers in the war did something similar. They all collected some kind of trophy. The mentality always was either to conquer or be conquered. The law of the strong shall prevail. This sort of thinking kept the men alive, as they knew that their own days were numbered. Many men of all nationalities died in the war. Some were as young as fifteen (who enlisted themselves to serve their country by claiming they were eighteen). My sister met many people during our stay in Volujak that were in the military.

Bruno, one of her friends, recommended my sister (fifteen at the time) to work as a waitress in a Croatian bar in Kreševo. We did not have much money—not enough to just once in a while get ten KM from my mother's work—so we needed to find other job opportunities. My sister did not work there for long—maybe a couple of weeks. Bruno even gave her a pistol and showed her how to shoot in case the drunk Croatian soldiers tried to make a move on her. Many of the soldiers were consistently drunk and high. While going off to battle, they were given moderate to high doses of different drugs to keep them calm under pressure. Some claimed that they did not even remember most days out on the battlegrounds due to the numbing of the mind and other side effects of the drugs.

Needless to say, war is always brutal. There is nothing fair or just about what any of the armies did. In other places, things were much worse—rapes of women and children. Kidnappings and forced selling of organs. In a lot of ways, we were lucky, even though we ourselves witnessed many atrocities. I was fortunate enough not to directly witness events like the rest of my family; I was protected from it as much as I could be. Me and my cousins. I did see the critically injured and various dead bodies being carried on stretchers to a nearby hospital and burial ground, but, apart from that, I was spared. For years, I was extremely sensitive to loud noises such as sirens, bombs exploding, and gunshots, but that faded away with time. The atrocities of war are not something that can be easily forgotten for most survivors. The PTSD from the war is a real thing for many people, even today in Bosnia and Herzegovina. The hypervigilance and the paranoia remain, along with the memories.

XIII
The Radio Station

Several months had passed rather quickly. One evening, our other family members joined us at the dinner table. It was a lovely occasion to have us all together in one place. We had an old radio that my mother would listen to a few times a week for updates on the war situation as well as for any announcements on any living or dead soldiers so their families could make peace with themselves—accept reality, in other words.

It is important that I go back several months in order to make sense of how the upcoming news changed things for us. My grandfather received news from one of his friends that my father got killed on the battlefield. When he received this news, he came for a visit and brought my mother two big cartons of cigarettes. He told my mother the entire story, and our mother sat us down that evening to tell us that our father had been killed and that from then on she was our mother and our father. We all cried and grieved our father's death for months. After some time, we accepted this and moved on to the best of our ability. Now let me return to what I mentioned at the beginning of this chapter.

So, that evening, as we all listened to the war announcements (one list was for the surviving or imprisoned soldiers, the second was for the killed soldiers), we received news that my father was imprisoned in Breza and alive! We had to verify that with everyone in the room to make sure that they heard my father's name: Tomislav Miletovic. My mother asked if there was another

Tomislav Miletovic out there, shocked and bewildered. She could not believe the news for days. My grandmother, along with my mother, went to the army station by bus to make sure that it was actually my father and her husband. They received confirmation that, indeed, it was *the* Tomislav Miletovic. As my sister and I were celebrating and screaming for joy—tears and all—that same evening, we found out that my Aunt Dražana's husband and my two cousins' father was killed by a grenade. Here, the three of us were celebrating, and, at the same time, the others were crying. I will never forget this whirlwind of mixed emotions. We all loved Goran dearly (one of the reasons why I included a chapter with his name). His death was difficult for all of us, and it took us all a long time to accept his fate. He was only thirty years old. A beautiful soul gone from this world.

When my father got released with some of the other soldiers close to the end of the war (late 1994), he was told that his family was located in Volujak and that they would be waiting for him there. My sister was the one that received the news that our father was released (from a friend of hers whose father held a high position), and we waited for the day we would see our father again. When the morning came, I remember my mother telling us to get dressed and brush our teeth. One of my mother's friends drove us to the station. My heart was pounding out of my chest. I was so excited and nervous at the same time. When we got there, we had to wait in a long line (other families were there too). There was a building not too far from us, and that was where we saw men in different uniforms—young and old. When our turn came, one of the soldiers called my father's name, and a skinny man with a shaved head appeared in front of us. I did not recognize the man in front of me. My body was frozen. My mother and my sister said, "Sanda, it is your dad. Go!" When the man said my name, I recognized the voice and remembered that that man was my dad! He smiled at me, and I ran to him, and he held me up and raised me up to the sky. The feeling that I felt in that moment cannot be captured in words. I was just so happy that my father was alive and that he was back in our lives after not seeing him for two years. I would lie if I said that his 'death' did not affect me for months on end, and his coming back to my life again was something that needed to be slowly integrated into my psyche again. Back from the dead to the land of the living.

XIV
The UN Tanks

Shortly after the war officially ended, the United Nations settled in Bosnia and Herzegovina in different regions. We had several troops in Kiseljak that would also pass by Kreševo and Volujak. We would know they were coming through by the loud sounds their tanks would make. Our house would be shaking at times as the enormous tires would roll on the road. The UN for us kids was something to look forward to every week as they would throw us toys and chocolate out of their tanks. My cousins and I would try to catch as many as we could. Sometimes, they would even throw cigarettes and money, which was a treat for our families.

The UN troops we would see in the town were from Canada and the Netherlands. Many of them I remember were tall and strong, often smiling at the townspeople. Their purpose was to distribute food and keep peace between all of the nationalities in the country. I believe they stayed for a whole twelve months, and then they departed back to their countries of origin. My family was always suspicious of the UN (what they wanted from us), but I think, for me, I just saw them as people and not as something menacing. People in general had many theories about the UN's involvement and NATO in general. Some were good and some were bad, as most things in life. I prefer to stay away from discussing politics, especially since I was a child then, and also because I think politics always complicates things. Instead of simplifying our lives, politics just complicates them more.

My cousin Bruno one day was asked to ride in the UN tank by one of the Canadian soldiers since we would see him quite often walking to the 'downtown' area of town. I wanted to go too, so I indicated my wish using somewhat broken sign language. He understood and climbed me up on top of the tank as well. He played some English music—country—and Bruno and I were so happy to be in a tank. He did not take us far. Maybe a ten-minute tank ride. After the ride, the same soldier gave us ice cream and sent us on our way. We told our families what had happened, and they were extremely angry with us. They told us we could have been kidnapped, sold, raped, killed, etc. We laughed it off and said that they were being paranoid. Actually, now come to think of it, many years later, they had a good point. Many children, especially young girls, were taken advantage of by everyone who held a high position (police, army, etc.). There were various scandals concerning the UN that Katherine Bolkovac uncovered in the late 2000s. Prostitution rings and many other series of crimes were investigated, and finally justice was served—not without tremendous efforts from willing women and men.

Regardless of the dangers, my family still held on to the belief that the majority of people are good and that in order for us all to get along, we would need to trust each other and come to some sort of arrangement where all parties are satisfied. I think that there was a great fear of losing more people we loved—we already grieved enough as it was. The only priority mothers had was to keep their children safe at all times. Even years later, my mother and her sisters had a desire to control our whereabouts, which was something that created a lot of disagreements and misunderstandings. We kids could not understand why our mothers were so dominant and controlling, but it explains a lot now that we are older and we can see the world more through their eyes.

3. POST-WAR

XV
Medi and Keti

While living in Volujak for almost two years now, my sister and I stumbled upon a ginger kitten while walking home from the convenience store. The kitten was meowing in the bushes, and we saw that it was alone. Its mother was nowhere to be found. Afraid that it would get hit by a car, I took it in my sweater and carried it home. My mother welcomed it pleasantly, and we fed it milk and gave it some tuna. It devoured the whole thing and then fell asleep in a little house we made for it, with an overused towel and an old doll house. This kitten grew into a beautiful feline. I cannot remember how we came up with the name Keti for it; I think it was actually our father who named it.

Our parents' friends' had a dog that would visit us from time to time. Medi (his name) followed us home once, and he never forgot how to get to our house—always back and forth between his actual owners and our family. Medi was injured during the war; his left leg was a bit shorter than his right one, but he was definitely a trooper! The happiest dog we ever encountered. He and Keti got along well. Keti (female) would sleep beside him, sometimes on him.

I remember walking home with my cousin Bruno and seeing both Medi and Keti running toward us. They would both do this if they recognized any of us. We would pet them and give them a small treat to show our appreciation. We truly loved these animals, and they were part of our family. Eventually, Medi died of old age, and Keti herself too—but not without having a litter of her own. She gave birth in a barn to a total of five kittens. Unfortunately, only one survived. A small tuxedo. We took him in, and he stayed with us. We kept feeding him milk and kitty formula. He grew up rather quickly and would join his mom on hunting adventures. Cico was his name.

One day, while visiting our grandparents, we were followed by a small poodle mix. It would not leave us alone. I asked my parents if we could keep it; it was dirty and looked malnourished. There was no collar on it. With much reluctance from my father, my mother ended up convincing him to take in that little poodle mix. We fed it, and it stayed with us for several months. Eventually, his real owners took him back, paying us a nice chunk of money. My sister and I were sad to see Lily (the dog's name) go, but we were also happy that it had a good home to go back to.

I often think back on my happy memories with all these pets we had. My love for animals and my dedication to helping them find decent homes followed me into adulthood. My sister and I ended up owning other animals after we left Bosnia and Herzegovina. I know there are still animals who are abandoned there on a daily basis. I try not to think about it too much because it makes me cry. Finally, in the last five years or so, there have been animal organizations that are addressing these issues, and the Bosnian government is adapting stricter laws and harsher penalties for animal abandonment and abuse in the country.

XVI
Shenanigans

In the spring and summer time, my cousins and I would build small rockets out of aluminum foil, matches, and small fireworks. We would let them explode in the middle of the road at night. We would compete with each other—who could build one the fastest. There was another boy that joined our gang, and his name was Vedran. Vedran moved in with his parents across the road from our house. In the morning, we would see Vedran peeing outside his house. It was hilarious! He felt no shame and was proud of his package (what he would say). We were all about eight years old at this point, except for my cousin Bruno, who was ten years old. I remember we found an abandoned barn one day, and Vedran got the idea in his head that we could climb to the top of the roof and jump into the hay. And guess what? That's exactly what we did. None of us considered the consequences. We just lived in the moment!

On another occasion, we stole a bike from a rich girl and took it home with us. It was a very nice bike. Neither of us cared that it was pink—for girls. We took turns riding it, and then Vedran's mother and my mother yelled at us for taking it in the first place. We had no other choice but to return it and apologize to the family. We were so mad at our parents for taking 'our' bike away. This was where we learned that theft was not okay. We were bitter and resentful for weeks. The girl that owned the bike was not a nice girl, so we felt justified in taking it away from her.

In downtown Volujak, there lived three sisters. My cousin Bruno had a crush on the middle sister, whereas Vedran was in love with the youngest sister. I liked the oldest sister. I guess there was no competition between us! We would hang out with them quite often. I think Bruno even ended up dating the middle sister for a few weeks. I listened to the older sister talk about her studies and what she was looking for in a boy, while at the same time I fantasized about being with her in a romantic way. Since I assumed that everyone felt the same feelings as I did, it never occurred to me until my teenage years that no, that was not the case. I kept my feelings to myself, so I never expressed them verbally to someone. I was just having fun imagining situations and living in my own world.

We still continued looking for empty shells in the forest nearby. At one point, we even collected unused medical syringes—small, medium, and large sizes. I had a full plastic bag of them. We would fill them with water and go on a full-blown war against each other. That was fun! Truly, we were free to be ourselves. Nobody controlled us (unless necessary), and we would roam free, visiting the hills and forests. I also remember building small huts from the materials we had gathered. We had a saw and some other tools to help us build what we wanted. We encountered deer, wild dogs, stray cats, and eagles. In fact, we found an eagle nest and fed the babies regularly. The parents rarely showed up, so we felt it was our responsibility to feed these babies. Eventually, the babies grew up and flew away. We were proud that we were the ones to have been there for them.

XVII
School

I completed Grade 1 and Grade 2 in Volujak. The elementary school was located in a designated area of Volujak called Polje (space in English). I would walk there and back by myself; it was a twenty-five-minute walk one way. Since none of us had a car (too expensive) in my family, we did a lot of walking. My cousins went to an elementary school in Kiseljak. We did not see each other that much except on the occasional weekend.

The school curriculum was demanding. I remember memorizing a lot of poems by heart and reciting them in front of the class. One of the poems was entitled 'Junak of Boga,' or 'Hero of God.' It was two pages long, and if we did not get the entire thing right, we would not pass. My Grade 1 teacher's name was Sonja. She was a beautiful young woman; needless to say, I had a huge crush on her. She had long brown hair and brown eyes. She would always come in with a smile to greet us, and we would all stand up to show our respect. She would bring us a large bag of apples on Fridays, and we would eat them during lunch. She was kind like that. I do remember that I received a 1 (equivalent to an F) on one of her math tests. I did not care much for math class; I loved art, drama, science, and music. I always dreaded math lessons. Sonja told me to show my mother the test and to make sure that she signs it. I knew that my mother would be angry with me, so I asked my sister to forge her signature. And she agreed only if I would do some of her chores during the week.

53

We were sneaky like that.

My Grade 2 teacher was another story. He was a proud Croatian, and, on the first day of class, he told us how we would respond with our fingers (to give answers in class). Josip (his name) told us that we must raise two fingers because that indicates we are Croatians and that we must never raise three fingers (Serbians) or the whole hand (Bosniaks). How fascist was that! I was left puzzled, along with my other classmates. It was such a bizarre speech coming from our new teacher. We all hopelessly wanted Sonja to be back and teach us. Sonja did not stay at our school after Grade 1. I am not sure where she went or what happened to her. She will always remain my Miss Honey (*Matilda* reference). My friend Oliver and I would skip class quite often. We would go and play soccer in the fields and tell our parents that we had a good day at school. Honestly, I am not sure how we passed Grade 2. I suppose we did the minimum, and the rest was history. I did make some good friends at the school. We would play skip rope and tag during recess, and we would draw with different-colored chalks all over the sidewalks. I enjoyed school, but what I enjoyed more was doing something else afterward. How did I become a teacher in my adult years? I suppose having a teacher like Sonja piqued my interest in the subject of education.

XVIII
Canada

We never imagined leaving our home country, but we did in 1995. My father, due to his time as a Bosnian Croat soldier, was given an opportunity to move to another country and start a new life. While spending several months in Zagreb, Croatia, my father gathered all of the required documents that our family needed to file for landed immigrant status. When all of us attended a scheduled meeting in Zagreb with the embassy/consulate, the lady gave us three choices: Australia, the U.S.A., and Canada. They were quite specific in their description. Australia was available for mixed-nationality marriages (so a Bosnian Croat and a Bosnian Serb), the U.S.A. was much of the same, and, lastly, Canada accepted all. Our father chose Canada, and that was that. My mother agreed with his decision while my sister and I were trying to locate Canada on the globe in the office.

After a month had passed, my mother picked up the documents through the Volujak post office, and we were officially given the green light. My sister did not want to leave for Canada as she had to leave her boyfriend Daniel behind. She took it the hardest. I, on the other hand, saw it as a new adventure. Yes, I was sad that we were leaving our extended family, but, as my mother explained to us, this was our big chance to go out in the world and have a better life. Truthfully, there would not have been much of a life for us if we stayed in Volujak. My father had his eye on Canada, and he told us that he was doing this so we could succeed in life. He would say to people, since he has two daughters, that all he wants for us is to become the best versions of ourselves in a country that embraces diversity and equality.

When the day finally arrived for us to leave Volujak, our entire family came to our house and brought us small gifts, money, and several photos for us to have on our new journey. We all had tears in our eyes because we did not know when we would see each other again. We were leaving all of it behind, and now we would be stepping into the unknown, with limited knowledge of English and absolutely no French. My sister and I sat at the back of the van that picked us up, and as we turned around, our family was waving to us as our cousins ran after the van, trying to catch up with us. There is a photo out there somewhere of all of us together before our departure to North America. I believe it is in one of my aunt's albums.

THE END